Smart Journaling

How to Form Life-Changing Journal Writing Habits that Actually Work for Reaching Any Goal and Getting Your Life on Track

Smart Journaling in Short

Smart journaling is writing down whatever is in the inner recesses of your mind and doing something to make it tangible. It is how goals are achieved and dreams are turned into reality.

It gives you a basic structure that you can work with because it allows you the flexibility to customize the system to match your purpose. It directs you to the right path and if you stray too far, it steers you right back.

It is this book's intention to arm you with the tools necessary to achieve success in all aspects of your life through journaling.

Table of Contents

Introduction

Journal writing has been around for ages, but people are now re-discovering its usefulness. It's easy to underestimate the value of journal writing as a powerful tool because you have been told that it's just a log of feelings, thoughts, and observations about events of the day. It's just a record of scribblings and musings for other people to read long after you are gone. It's like a time capsule for future people to find and dissect.

If you still believe in this archaic view of journal writing, then you are missing out on an important productivity tool that could change your life exponentially.

It is time to wrap your head around the idea that journal writing can be an effective system to improve your life and reach important goals and milestones. When you do this, you are one step closer to achieving a more productive version of yourself.

In this book of 13 chapters, each chapter tackles different concepts, theories, ideologies, and systems that explain the rationale and importance of smart journaling. The structure of the book is designed to gain a better understanding of why some of your habits and actions stop you from being productive. These very same habits are the obstacles that are holding you back from achieving your goals in life.

Journal writing is not a new concept at all, but not many people are aware that it is a valuable tool to help complete even the most difficult tasks and achieve even the most ambitious goals. It has to be emphasized that all the good things cannot be achieved by just writing down thoughts. There must be a corresponding action as well. Smart journaling addresses this issue and fills in the gaps for the activity to serve a more substantial purpose.

Chapter 1 tells you why it makes sense to get into journaling. The practice has been trivialized many times over and this Chapter convinces you of the many benefits that you can get out of smart journaling.

Chapter 2 explains the science behind distraction and how it affects our productivity. It offers ways on how to manage distraction through the use of smart journaling.

Chapter 3 discusses the reasons why you can't stay focused on one thing and why there is a need to use journaling as a way to declutter your mind.

Chapter 4 introduces the basics of smart journaling and how one does not need to work harder to reap the benefits of journal writing.

Chapter 5 presents the different types of journal writing approaches that one can choose from. Each one of them addresses a certain journaling need. One can choose one approach or a combination of approaches depending on the goals.

Chapter 6 explains the evils of procrastination and what interventions can be done to stop it on its tracks. The solutions, of course, include journaling.

Chapter 7 introduces the Bullet Journal created by Ryder Carroll. It explains how it works and how its simplicity can make journaling more efficient and fun.

Chapter 8 introduces Dot Journaling, an offshoot of the Bullet Journal. It shows different ways to customize a journal using layouts, symbols, signifiers, and other journaling elements

Chapter 9 discusses the intricacies of goal-setting and how to create SMART goals, so you can set yourself up for true success.

Chapter 10 presents what needs to be done to levelling up in all aspects of life. It provides exercises and examples on how to set up goals for the 10 main focus areas of life.

Chapter 11 emphasizes on training the brain and linking up goals to brain exercises for maximum focus.

Chapter 12 lists and reviews some of the more popular pre-made journal templates to help users choose the most appropriate one and so that they can get started sooner than later.

Chapter 13 provides an example of smart journaling by combining Bullet Journal and Dot Journaling and applying the theories, ideas, and concepts discussed in the book.

At the end of this book is a list of sources and references to help you expand the knowledge and understanding that you have gained about smart journaling.

This book hopes to encourage people to use the power of smart journaling for self-discovery, mental inventory, and goal-setting. There are different approaches and methods to start a smart journaling routine and some of them will be discussed in detail. It does not matter what method you choose; the important thing is to get started right now.

Chapter 1

Making Sense of Journaling

The old way of journaling is to write whatever comes to mind. There were no rules and no limitations. It's essentially a freestyling activity that is done without a specific purpose. While there is nothing wrong with that approach, it's just all over the place. It's like a scatterbrained friend who is easily distracted by just about anything. There's just no focus. Instead of getting some clarity of thought, you end up with a lot of noise. Instead of decluttering your mind, you are encumbered by things that are not vital to the achievement of your goals.

If journaling is counterproductive, then why should you even bother doing it? Because journaling has an inherent value when used with an outcome in mind. Outcomes are results that you want to achieve for yourself. It can be about personal growth, financial independence, physical transformation, or spiritual enlightenment. It can be anything you desire that improves your overall well-being or a breakthrough that you've been waiting for all your life.

Putting "intention" into the journal writing equation makes the effort worthwhile. You are setting yourself up for success by arming yourself with the right mindset and clear focus. You save time and energy, which are two things that people always complain that they do not have enough of. When stress and anxiety are removed from the equation, or at least brought down to a minimum, then you have room to focus on the essentials of life.

If you're still not convinced that smart journaling is a powerful tool, keep reading...

Smart Journaling Gives You a Mental Inventory

When you write about your thoughts, feelings, and observations about something or someone, you are taking stock of your mental disposition. It gives you a moment to assess where you are at mentally. You have a better understanding of why you feel a certain way or why you do the things that you do. What this does is to make you much more in tune with your emotions and values. As a result, you can easily determine what matters to you. Things that do not connect to you in a meaningful way are just mental clutter and have to go.

Smart Journaling Gives the Mind Room to Think

It's easy to be overwhelmed by the daily grind up to the point of feeling suffocated and exhausted by life's daily dose of stress and anxiety. What smart journaling does is to get things organized in a way that best suits your daily routine. It gets rid of the things that do not have any bearing on your ultimate goal in life. With less stress, the mind is able to think with more clarity.

Smart Journaling Improves Mental Focus

A direct result of having mental clarity is improved focus. When faced with multiple tasks, it's easy to become overwhelmed and you start to lose focus. Smart journaling helps you prioritize your tasks and complete them systematically and efficiently, instead of fumbling your way through each task.

Smart Journaling Improves Insight

A clear mind makes you more receptive to new insights. You become more aware of other possibilities and perceptions. Insights that you would have otherwise missed would surface, which gives you a better understanding of yourself and of others.

Smart Journaling Leads to Problem Solving

With mental clarity, the mind opens itself to more solutions to different problems. You are able to weigh the choices and apply the process of elimination. When presented with more options, you stand to choose the best possible solution to a problem. This is because the mind is in its best condition to sort through the information it is presented with.

Smart Journaling Tracks Personal Growth and Development

Writing down experiences on a daily basis allows you to become more aware of small daily milestones. These are small victories that you tend to overlook or pay no attention to because they are being eclipsed by bigger and more significant life events. When you read what you have written, you can see how much you've grown as a person by learning from mistakes and missteps. One day you wake up and you wonder how you've come this far and all you have to do is revisit your journal entries to find your answers.

Smart Journaling Sets You Up for Success

When you journal with a purpose, you are preparing yourself to accomplish the goals that you set up. You are utilizing a powerful tool that is designed to make you succeed. It not only maps out your life's journey, it also equips you with the necessary tools to get you from one point to the next until you get close to achieving your ultimate goal in life.

Smart journaling is the evolved version of journal writing of olden days. It is a means to an end and a simple tool that can solve even the most complex life problems. All it takes is a notebook, a pen, and your mind.

Chapter 2

Too Many Distractions, Too Many Things to Do

There is a tendency for people today to blame the internet for their inability to focus on the things that they need to accomplish. Social media is perceived as the evil distraction that curtails productivity. But social media is just a tiny portion of what distracts you.

A distraction can be anything that takes away your attention from what you are supposed to be doing in the first place. With the emergence of new technology, you are inundated by more information than what your brain is used to. In most cases, simply just can't keep up. You feel overwhelmed and are unable to perform a task satisfactorily. You lose your focus.

When you focus on something, your brain increases the processing of information that are relevant to you. Conversely, it decreases the processing of those that are irrelevant to you. Remember that your brain is not wired to focus on more than one complex task at a time. It's just not possible to place the same level of attention to several things when you're attempting to do them at the same time. That's the reason why you should not text and drive or operate machinery while meditating. Something's gotta give.

Attention is a Scarce Resource

Science explains that the human brain can only focus on one task at a time. Even when you multitask, you are not focusing on all the tasks simultaneously. You are just simply shifting your focus from one task to the next at a rapid pace. This is because your attention is limited.

Every time you focus your attention on something, you are using up energy in the form of glucose and metabolic resources. Physically, you are spent after completing a task. When you move on to the next task, you have less energy and are more likely to become less effective, more overwhelmed, and more mentally fatigued. Imagine just how much energy you are wasting when you shift your focus to one distraction after another.

Distraction Takes a Heavy Toll on Productivity

With endless distractions, it would take ages to finish a task that could normally be done in a short time. When you are easily distracted, you spend more time and energy than what is required to complete a particular task.

Studies have shown that it takes 25 minutes to get back to the original task after being interrupted or distracted. So, if you keep switching activities, your ability to stay focused drops considerably because you have less energy to spend. You have less capacity to understand, recall, memorize, or decide. And this is the moment when your productivity level takes a nosedive.

Managing Distractions

By now, you should be convinced that distractions steal your limited supply of attention. You need to be mindful of what you should be focusing your attention on. Of course, you need to be realistic as well since distractions will always rear their ugly heads.

You just need to choose the right amount of distractions that you allow to creep into your daily activities. Managing distractions entails learning how to focus by decluttering the mind, which will be addressed by the Zen-like process of smart journaling.

Chapter 3

From Scatterbrain to Hyper Focus

A person is inundated by over 70,000 thoughts daily. There's a whole lot of thinking going on inside your head. It's like Los Angeles traffic during rush hour in there. It's just too crowded. It's no wonder that you have lost the ability to focus on what really matters to you. You switch focus depending on what catches your fancy, never mind if they are completely irrelevant to your existence and totally unrelated to your life goals.

You have to realize that you are focusing on the wrong things, that's why you are easily overwhelmed when you are faced with challenges and difficulties. This is how you end up making wrong decisions that steer your life in the wrong direction.

Every day, people make big and small decisions that could affect the course of their lives. You make decisions based on the information that you have. In this day and age, information flows non-stop from various sources. Processing all these information is nearly impossible, so you take only what you can and hope for the best.

At times, it becomes too overwhelming, that you avoid making decisions altogether. You are crippled with stress and anxiety and you feel like losing control of your life. But it does not have to be that way. You can do better because you have the tools to make mid-course corrections to improve the quality of your life. And it all starts by ditching Scatterbrain Sally and embracing Hyper Focus Henny.

Mental Decluttering

Think of it as the spring cleaning of the mind. It's clearing out the mental cobwebs and dust bunnies that have been living inside your head to free up some space and give your mind room to think and focus.

The way to do this is to write down what you need to do, what you should be doing, and what you want to do. Things that do not fall under these three categories are distractions that are not vital to achieving your goals. Hence, they must be thrown away. You should be left only with the things that you can work with and can focus on.

Mental Inventory

After freeing up your much-needed mental space, you will find yourself having more room to think and focus on the things that you should be accomplishing. You are left with information that you can manage with ease and will not make you feel overwhelmed or out of control. But even with the very best intentions, there's always the risk of falling back to the old habit of switching focus.

Distractions are everywhere, so if you are not completely committed to the goal, you'll once again start to accumulate non-vital information that would take up space in your mental pantry. To remedy this, it is important to keep track of your mental inventory and regularly update it so that you do not drift back to distractions that sabotage your progress and development.

Forming the Habit

Changing from a scatterbrain to hyper focus requires a bit of effort and takes a lot of getting used to. It takes repetition to form a habit. It can take a few days to weeks to months. It varies from person to person so don't feel like you're failing when it's taking you longer to get into the habit. You will get there if you just stick to the plan. It's just a matter of breaking bad habits and forming good ones.

Chapter 4

Journaling Smarter, Not Harder

Journaling is easy. You just pick up a pen and notebook and you're good to go. There's not much preparation needed because you just write what you want. There's no right or wrong way of journaling because it's a personal activity that you are emotionally invested in. No one can say that you're doing it wrong because it is your own experience that's being written. But here's the thing, if you're writing complex entries, you're expending more energy than what's necessary that it becomes counterproductive. If it starts becoming a chore, it sucks out the fun of doing it and you're likely to abandon the activity altogether.

Traditional journal writing is hard work because they are very detailed. Events are described as they happened, so they are loaded with information, some of which may not be necessary. At times, there's more fluff than useful information. The time and effort to chronicle the day's events can be exhausting in itself, so you have less time, less energy, and less interest in doing everything else. There's no benefit in that.

Journaling with a Purpose

Journal writing has always been done with a purpose. Traditionally, the purpose is to record events that include the author's thoughts and observations. There's no intent to declutter the mind or clarify life goals. It's a straightforward recording of events from a person's point of view. There's a lack of structure and the organization can be fuzzy.

If you start a journal with an intention to accomplish something, it's called intentional journaling. Your intention creates a structure that you can work with. It gets you on track because the path is cleared out for you and you can focus on that journey.

Intentional journaling helps promote a purposeful living. It's the foundation where our pursuit of happiness is built on. An intentional journal serves as a roadmap to organizing your life and becoming a more productive individual. Of course, there are many paths to a goal, but if you establish some form of a system, you can avoid confusion and chaos as you navigate life. And if you lose your way, which is possible, you can find your way back with less difficulty.

Reflective Writing

Smart journaling is reflective writing that engages your mind more deeply into the information that is available to you. This kind of engagement increases your self-awareness because you now have the propensity to look deeper into your own character, emotions, feelings, motivations, and desires. You are able to focus on yourself in such a way that you evaluate your current behavior against your inner values and standards. You learn about yourself without judgment and without being hard on yourself. This kind of self-awareness is the cornerstone to understanding yourself, so you can be proactive in managing your behavior.

Setting Compelling Goals

Tony Robbins has long been emphatically preaching the importance of having a crystal-clear goal to create a compelling future. You know that this is a fundamental requirement to achieving success, and you have set goals at one point or another. But have you ever stopped and wondered why some people succeed in life and others stumble despite setting up their goals? The answer is right there under your nose — ineffective goal setting.

It's one thing to set a goal and it's another to set a goal that excites you to your very core. There is no point in setting a goal that doesn't make you come alive. It has to be a goal that would make you wake up each day bursting with positive energy to face the day's challenges. Your goal has to be bigger than just achieving it. It has to transform you in ways you didn't know were possible.

According to Robbins, the first step in goal setting is to brainstorm and create a list of all the things that you want to achieve for the next 20 years. These are long-term goals that can pertain to any aspect of your life. You can write as many or as little as you like as long as they are truly your goals. It can be something you want to create, something you want to achieve, something you want to improve, or something you want to experience, among other things. There's no limit to the items in your list and there are no wrong entries.

The second step is to assign a deadline for each goal. Go through your list and decide how long it will take to achieve those goals. Don't take too long to do this. Give yourself a few minutes. The next step is to review your list and choose the top four or five goals that really excite you. It's important to explain why and how you plan to achieve your top goals in the next 12 months. It's a way of committing to the goals you've set for yourself.

You should also allot time to assess how you're progressing with your goals. This is where daily journal writing plays a pivotal role. Write down your goals and take an action each day that will bring you closer to achieving them.

Creating Your Own System

If you're new to journaling, you might feel a little lost because there are many suggestions and recommendations on how to get started — from what notebooks to use to what pens work best with what type of paper to what entries to write. The list of options is enough to overwhelm you.

If all the hype is too much for you, just start out simple. Get a notebook and a pen and just write your goals and keep track of your progress. If you'd rather use journaling for something else, then go with it. Nobody said you have to follow other people's rules.

You set your own rules and create your own system. Remember, journaling is an activity that involves you and the journal and no one else. The system has to work for you and it should be customized to cater to your needs. Forget other people's journals and focus on how you want your journal to be. Your journal, your rules.

Finding Tools

Creating your own journaling system doesn't mean that you can't use existing systems for inspiration or guidance. From all the suggestions you've collected, choose one or a combination of systems that you think would work best for your purpose. You can also use tools to help you. These tools can be in the form of apps, templates, prompts, exercises, or writing sprints.

If you feel that the tools you have chosen are not working after you've given them a reasonable amount of time, then by all means, scout for other more useful tools. Get the advice of people who have been journaling for so long and are experiencing success. Sometimes, you need to go directly to these people to have a better understanding of the tools that they utilize.

You may even find tips and tricks on how to properly execute some tasks that you have trouble completing. Journal writing is a personal journey, but finding help is a communal activity. You learn more from people who have been there and done that.

Chapter 5

Choose Your Journaling Jam

Now that you know the rationale, motivations, and benefits of smart journaling, it's time to get started. But, before you get to the fun part, you first have to find out what types of journals you can use. Smart journaling has no strict rules. You're pretty much in control of the journaling situation. You can choose one approach or a combination of approaches that will match your personality, interests, or goals.

Keep in mind that you are not limited to just one form of journal writing. Free writing is completely fine if that's your jam, but you'd be surprised to know that certain goals fit certain journal approaches. And that's where the fun part usually comes in. For starters, here are some of the most popular structures to whet your journal writing appetite.

The Goal Journal

This approach is for those who want to achieve something. There is a specific outcome in mind and the objectives are clear. This is not merely listing down what your goals are, but rather incorporating them into your day-to-day activities. The goals can be the simple but immediate goals that you want to get done in within the week or they can be much more difficult such that they take months or years to achieve. This is the approach to take if you are keen on losing weight, acquiring something of value, or achieving milestones.

You can also have goals that are intangible in nature. The outcomes are not measurable in a strict sense, but they are improvements in certain aspects of your life. It can be related to improving your social skills, working on your personal relationships, or developing better relations at work.

Apart from your goals, the journal also includes progress updates. This is the part where you take the time to keep track of the progress so far. It makes you aware of the obstacles that are stopping you from achieving your goals, so adjustments can be done if some things are not working out.

The Gratitude Journal

Appreciation enables the mind to focus on the positive things. Expressing gratitude creates a whole spectrum of positive emotions that can lead to happiness. People who are aware of the power of gratitude know that they can unlock the secret to having a happier life. With that in mind, having a gratitude journal is a commitment to become a happier person. Studies have shown that writing down what you are grateful for compensates for the brain's tendency to focus on negative thoughts like worry, anxiety, angst, and apprehension.

The gratitude journal must focus on the events that really have an impact on your life. Writing down every little thing seems superficial and the perceived benefits may wear off.

The Ideas Journal

Some of the best ideas are written on napkins, sticky notes, or crumpled pieces of paper because you never know when inspiration strikes so you jot down ideas on something that was readily available at that moment. Keeping an idea journal allows you to list down all the ideas that come to mind the moment they hit you. Needless to say, you have to take the journal wherever you go, so no small or big idea is left unwritten.

This approach entails a second step wherein at the end of the day, you have to review what you've written and decide which of the ideas are more likely to stick. Keep the ideas that help you discover new solutions to problems and give deeper insights into certain situations.

Reflecting on written thoughts and ideas can help you draw a wider understanding of whatever is impacting your life at the moment. Apart from this, you are able to create new things that can help you advance your career. This journal is perfect for artists, inventors, and anyone who loves creating new things.

The Values Journal

As previously mentioned, developing self-awareness allows you to reflect on your values and standards. Keeping a values journal enables you to connect the events of the day to your personal values. Journaling, in this sense, takes on a much more significant purpose as you are able to manage stressful situations because you are able to act and decide based on the values and standards that you abide by.

The first step in starting your values journal is to identify the values that are truly important to you. This can be done by creating your very own personal mission statement, writing it on your journal, using it as the cornerstone of your reflection as you write down each entry.

The Curiosity Journal

They say that curiosity killed the cat. While this is true for the most part, curiosity, when used with a good purpose in mind, can re-energize cognitive abilities. Scientifically speaking, a person who is continuously seeking out explanations and exploring new ideas possesses an active brain.

If you are constantly seeking out answers, you come across new ideas and learn from new experiences. An active brain creates a rich environment that is conducive to cultivating curiosity. The fun part of this activity is that you are challenging yourself by asking questions about the things that you notice every day.

The Project Journal

This type of journal is much more structured than most other approaches because you include things that are vital to the completion of a project. It includes the materials needed, the steps required, the people involved, and the budget required.

What this type of journal does is to capture important information so that the project does not go off tangent. In the process, you are able to manage the activities for your projet well. You also get to discover new ways of doing things that are more efficient, more effective, and less costly.

The Mindfulness Journal

Mindfulness is the keen awareness of the present moment. It means experiencing the present without judgment. It is the complete acceptance of what is happening at a point in time. Practicing mindfulness makes you regain control of yourself and your life. You become more aware of the more important things in your life and you're not easily distracted. It makes you focus better because you see through all the illusions and distractions.

The concept itself is a little difficult to grasp and it takes practice to get used to it. One way to master it is to keep a mindfulness journal. It serves to chronicle your dialogues with yourself, so you can be more sensitive of what is going on in the present.

The Morning Pages

This is also called 'Daily Pages' if you're not a morning person. Popularized by Julia Cameron, the Morning Pages is basically a daily three-page stream of consciousness longhand writing. There's only one rule: *Anything goes!*

Whoa! Wait a minute. Who has time for three pages of writing—and longhand too?

The ritual allows you to write anything that comes to mind without censoring your thoughts. This free flow of thoughts is mostly of the negative kind—frustrations, anxieties, worries, self-doubts, failures, and other things that hang over your head because they are not properly processed. Morning pages allows you to unload whatever is burdening you emotionally. This clears up your mind and makes room to focus on the day ahead.

The more you write, the more you discover things and uncover secrets that would not have been possible if your mind is bogged down by so much information. It's like emptying the mind of rubbish to make room for creativity and ingenuity.

But why longhand?

This might be difficult to understand at first, but the reasoning is simple. Longhand is slow and deliberate which connects people emotionally to what they are doing. Typing or texting may be easier and faster, but they don't give the same level of emotional connection.

Writing in the morning has a significant reason as well. According to Chris Winfield, the veil of the ego is at the thinnest in the morning and that's the best time to pour out all your feelings because your ego will not get in the way.

As with other journal approaches, you can try Morning Pages for a week and evaluate if the ritual makes you calmer and more productive.

The Creative Journal

Journals are only limited by your imagination. Some people are not very good at expressing themselves in words, so they use other creative means to do it. Creative journals have entries that contain illustrations, sketches, and diagrams, to name just a few. They are like scrapbooks that can represent significant moments or events from the creator's life and can be used as a fulfilling creative outlet. If you are a visual kind of person, a creative journal would appeal to you.

The Challenge Journal

Some people are driven by challenges. If they are not challenged, they will not make a move. That's why some people start making changes in their lives when there is something big at stake. There are also those who are motivated by financial rewards, fame, prestige, or just good old bragging rights. Others are motivated by anger. This is why 100-day challenges are so popular.

Goals are set within a short time-frame because there is some sort of gratification when you're seeing a huge progress in just a short amount of time. People have found ways to incorporate the element of challenge in journal writing and they have been reaping the benefits. Challenge journals are usually methodical and task-oriented because of the limited time element attached to them.

The presence of a deadline adds more pressure, which makes it more urgent for you to achieve the goals. What a challenge journal also does is to stop procrastination and unnecessary delays. It also limits distractions to a minimum because time is in short supply when you are participating in a challenge. The element of time and the desire to beat the time to achieve the goals are the main motivations that make challenge journals appealing to competitive people. Generally, it works, but you should also be mindful that your intentions are in the right place and not just solely motivated by competition.

***

These are just some of the popular approaches to journal writing. Some will work better than the others or they may not work at all. In many cases, those who embark in journaling find that a combination of these approaches works well because the path to achieving goals is not always linear. Sometimes, you have to try many approaches to get to the finish line.

Regardless of what approach you choose, you have to commit to stick to it. Don't be discouraged when there's a lack of progress or improvement on your first try. If you're not seeing the desired results, you can make some adjustments and tweak the approach. What works for others doesn't necessarily mean that it would work for you. You must also refrain from being too critical about yourself and about your chosen approach. Give it time to work.

Chapter 6

Maybe Later, Maybe Not

Much of what you do not get to do is because of procrastination. If you understand and realize what journaling can do to help you achieve your goals and realize your dreams, there's no reason why you should not get started already. Unless, of course, you're procrastinating.

Nothing happens when you don't get started. You cannot expect your dreams to come true when you haven't even started chasing them. Stop procrastinating on journaling. Get started now. If you tend to put of your tasks for 'maybe later,' journaling can help push you out of your rut and get you going on your tasks.

Everyone procrastinates, but not everyone is a procrastinator. This is the reality. Many of you reading this book are convinced that journaling is a worthwhile activity, but some of you are putting off doing it because you are thinking that maybe you'll do it later when inspiration strikes. So when it doesn't strike, you'll be forever in that space where nothing productive happens, which defeats everything this book is trying to establish.

Reasonable Delay vs. True Procrastination

It's important to understand what procrastination really is by comparing it to reasonable delay. When you're putting off doing something because of time constraints and the task is not a priority, it's a reasonable delay. On the other hand, true procrastination is deliberately and voluntarily delaying crucial tasks, despite knowing that it can be harmful. Poor time management can make the problem worse, but it's not the main reason why procrastination happens. According to researchers, the very foundation of procrastination is the inability to manage emotions.

Procrastination is a deep-seated problem. According to psychology professor Joseph Ferrari, time management has little to do with procrastination. You can't just tell the chronic procrastinators to get a move on and expect them to actually do it. That's not how it works inside the procrastinator's brain.

Self-Defeating Behavior

Procrastination may have short-term benefits in that those who practice it usually have lower levels of stress in the beginning because they are pursuing more pleasurable activities instead of doing serious work. But the costs of procrastination outweigh the temporary benefits. In the end, procrastinators suffer a worse fate than non-procrastinators. Sure, they complete the task, but they are far more stressed out and exhausted. The quality of the finished job also suffers.

Studies show that even if the variables change and the rewards are given, the procrastinators would not change their behavior all that much, which undermines their best efforts. Procrastinators also feel guilty, ashamed, and anxious for their delaying tactics, so they are stuck in a procrastination loop.

But many people not chronic procrastinators, so there's hope yet. It's not a hopeless case and there are ways to break out of the procrastination loop.

Interventions

Professor of Psychology Laura Rabyn offered some interventions that could help defeat procrastination or keep it at bay, at the very least.

1. Breaking up tasks into manageable levels. Completing tasks in stages can give a sense of accomplishment that encourages on-time completion of the next stages.

2. Counseling. The main goal of this intervention is to make the procrastinator recognize the fact that their self-sabotaging behavior compromises long-term goals for instant gratification.

3. Self-Imposed Deadline. This is a pre-commitment to do something. Not all tasks have deadlines, but it helps to set one to instill discipline and self-control when there are other activities that give a quick burst of pleasure.

4. Blocking Desirable Distractions. This involves self-regulation on the part of the procrastinators. Remember that you have control over the things that distract you. You can choose to ignore the distractions that are derailing your plans.

5. Mood Fixes. Since procrastination is an emotion-based anomaly, the intervention should target the root cause of the problem. If you're not in the mood to do a task, then find something worthwhile about the task to turn the negative emotion into something positive.

6. Self-Forgiveness. Procrastination carries with it an enormous feeling of guilt and shame. Procrastinators feel bad because they know that they could do more and they could do better. They end up being hard on themselves. Forgiving yourself after procrastination forces you to take

action so that you don't ever have the need to feel sorry or guilty about procrastinating.

Stopping Procrastination on its Tracks

Here's an exercise that can help you stop procrastination. The system enables you to understand the cost of procrastination. It makes you become aware of the negative consequences that should dissuade you from indulging in this self-sabotaging act.

1. *Identify a project, a task, a behavior, or anything you are procrastinating on.*

Example: I am procrastinating on my journaling.

Journaling is not easy because oftentimes it takes a lot of planning and brainstorming before you actually sit down and get started. You have to choose what type of journal to start and the materials to use. You need it to be creative and you have your own ideas of how it should look like and what should be in it. You spend time overthinking things until it becomes too tedious for you and you just put it off for when you have more time to think about it or when you find the right materials.

When you procrastinate on your journaling, what exactly is holding you back. It surely is not as simple as what notebook or pen to use. Perhaps you are afraid of 'getting personal' with yourself and putting your self-doubt, hesitations, and fear down in your journal. Perhaps its something else entirely. Only you have the answers.

As you can see from the first step of this exercise, you are not only able to identify the problem, you also discover why it is a problem. From this, you are acknowledging that procrastination is not always caused by distractions or laziness. There's a deeper reason and you just have to unearth it.

2. *Determine the cost of your procrastination.*

Example: Each day I am procrastinating, I am missing out on opportunities and holding myself back from achieving success.

There really is no rush since your journal is between you and yourself. But, then again, you are journaling for a purpose. Procrastination has a cost in the form of consequences. This is quite hard to illustrate because you cannot easily grasp the idea of loss or gain when you haven't even started. If anything, you're losing time or wasting time. But if you think of it in terms of opportunity cost, then you will begin to grasp the extent of the consequences.

In this example, an opportunity cost is the loss of a potential gain if you choose to procrastinate rather than to get started on journaling. This potential gain can take many forms depending on what kind of journal you want to have. If you are looking at a Goal Journal, you could be missing out on a chance to take advantage of something that can fast-track you towards your goal.

If you are planning on starting a Curiosity Journal, you might not be able to capitalize on a novel idea that you have just because you failed to put it down on paper and recognize it as great opportunity.

3. *Think of three concrete solutions to fix the problem.*

Example:

> 1. *I will get a notebook and a pen and sit down to get started on my journal.*
>
> 2. *I will devote my morning today to writing down my goal for the week in my journal.*
>
> 3. *I will track my progress daily and write my 'report' in my journal before I end my day.*

These three solutions are simple and doable. There's nothing overly ambitious. They are reasonable fixes that don't require much. Solution #2 puts urgency into the task with the commitment to get started 'today' rather than an open statement without any indication as to when you will act. Instead of procrastinating, you push yourself to do the task.

In solution #3, makes you accountable for results and prevents you from procrastinating further in the tasks that you have to do to achieve your weekly goals, and later on your bigger goals as well.

Procrastination is a self-inflicted wound that can have terrible consequences, not just on performance, quality of work, or emotional state, but it can also affect the overall well-being of the person. Being trapped in this kind of behavior actually delays you from living the life that you are supposed to live and prevents you getting ahead.

Chapter 7

Getting Your BuJo on

What the heck is BuJo and why should you care? In Chapter 5, the different types of journals and the approaches that cater to different journaling goals were explained. You also learned that you can choose one or choose all depending on the goals you wish to achieve. Whatever floats your boat is what you use. No judgments.

But there is one approach that has taken the journal writing community by storm. It's called Bullet Journal or BuJo. Created by Ryder Carroll, BuJo is essentially a system to help people get organized. The system is simple because it streamlines the process so that you can see your progress immediately. Everything that you need to get done is all in one place, which allows you to keep track of your calendar, to do lists, and goals with ease.

BuJo is simple but highly customizable, which means that every element of smart journaling can be applied using the

BuJo approach. It gets to the heart of what matters, that's why it's efficient and effective.

All you need to do is to remember the basic elements that provide a structure that you can work with. Once you master that, the rest is pretty much up to you

Again, it only requires a pen and a journal notebook. That is why many are wondering how something so simple can be so innovative.

Rapid Logging

The system does away with lengthy journal entries and instead utilizes bullet points, short sentences, topics, and page numbers. The point of rapid logging is to focus on the priorities.

Topics and Page Numbers

Topics are short descriptive titles that you write down everytime you start a journal entry. Page numbers are written so that you can create an index (or table of contents at the end).

Bullets

Short objective sentences are denoted by bullet points. Every bullet has three categories:

1. <u>Tasks</u> (denoted by a dot "•") – these are actionable items. There are three notations that describe the progress of the actionable times.

   X Task Completed

   > Task Migrated

   < Task Scheduled

2. <u>Events</u> (denoted by an "O" bullet") – these are activities that can be scheduled or recorded after they have occurred.

3. <u>Notes</u> (denoted by a dash —) – these are entries that are not immediately actionable. They are usually thoughts, ideas, and observations.

Signifiers

These are symbols that provide context to the events as represented by bullets.

1. Priority (*)

2. Inspiration (!)

3. Explore (denoted by an eye symbol)

You are by no means limited to just these three signifiers. As you get comfortable with the system, you can add more signifiers or change the symbols as you see fit.

The Index

This essentially serves as the table of contents of the journal. The Index is comprised of the topics and the corresponding pages in which they appeared in the journal. They are arranged as collections where page numbers can be in range or by individual page numbers.

Future Log

This consists of a task list and the date of future events that you have to attend to.

Monthly Log

This is the monthly log of activities using a calendar to track monthly activities. It's meant to be used as a reference point, so keep it short.

Daily Log

This is used for daily activities. This should be written as you go and not days ahead or after.

Migration

Remember this notation under *Bullets?*

> Task Migrated

You might be wondering what this is and how to use it. Here's how: After one month of journaling, review the tasks that are not yet completed and decide if they are still important enough to be carried forward to the next month. If so, you have to change them from *Task Scheduled* to *Task Migrated* and move them to the following month.

The BuJo system is unique because of its customizability. It can be used no matter what your purpose is for journal writing. This framework agrees with the objectives of smart journaling. And since it is customizable, it can be further simplified, expanded, tweaked, adjusted, and fine-tuned to make sure the system works for you.

Many of the smart journal examples that you see online use the BuJo system as a start-off point. With creativity, smart journaling can become a cross between a crafts project and a journal, which makes it both a fun and worthwhile activity.

You will also find that many of the exercises, prompts, drills, and mental sprints in this book complement the BuJo system.

Chapter 8

Dot Journaling

When journal writing became a worldwide obsession, bullet journaling became popular because of its simple and streamlined approach. It's straight to the point and it gets rid of unwanted noise that clutter the conventional journal. But some people have found the approach a little too simple that it lacks personality.

The creative types began adding their artistic flair into their journaling that the term "bullet journal" no longer describes what the approach represents. The structure was expanded to include other elements that are normally (and intentionally) left out in the streamlined version.

Soon, people started using just one single notebook to for their to-do lists, diary entries, calendar, and even random brain dumps. That's how dot journaling came into existence. It just makes sense to put everything in one place because it gives you a picture of what your life looks like at a particular moment, so they can act or decide accordingly.

Flexibility

Dot journaling is not only a repository of daily tasks, goals, and important activities, it also serves as a creative outlet for people who like to make it more personal through different layouts and designs. There's no right or wrong way to do it.

There are no strict rules for layouts — and this is where the beauty of dot journaling lies. You can be as minimalist or as elaborate as you wish in your layout. As long as the journal remains primarily a productivity tool and it helps you to organize your daily, weekly, or monthly tasks, then, by all means, go crazy with your layouts and designs.

It can vary each day, depending on your mood or the situation you're in. The flexibility that dot journaling brings is what makes the system easy to work with. At times, you can get bored by doing the same thing over and over, but the great thing is that you can switch things up. If you feel that something is not working, you can try another approach or maybe another layout. You can even make mistakes. It's that flexible.

Things You Need to Get Started with Dot Journaling

You really don't need much to get started. Just get a notebook and a writing material (pen or pencil) and you're off.

The type of notebook and pen to use is not really a critical issue because the content and purpose are the stars of the show. It's easy to get distracted by the nice pens and pretty notebooks, but they aren't as important as the actual journal writing itself. However, if you must know, there are at three main types of journal notebooks that can be used in dot journaling. They are:

1. Blank Page Notebook. This allows you complete control of the layout and design of your journal. It's a blank canvass that you can use to make the journal both a productivity tool and a work of art. This is

recommended for the creative types who want to go beyond the minimalist bullet journaling approach.

2. Dot-Grid Notebook. This is a notebook that has dot-grids instead of lines. I particularly use a dot-grid notebook for journal writing because I have trouble keeping my writing straight in the absence of lines and I couldn't be bothered using a ruler. This is recommended for people who want a bit of structure but also want maximum flexibility.

3. Pre-made Templates. These are notebooks that contain writing prompts and exercises to help your brain warm up. They are provided so you stay on course if your mind strays off a bit. This is recommended for people who want to get started but don't know how. It will definitely give them the boost they need to start dot journaling. There's an entire chapter on pre-made journal templates here because they are very useful. Check out Chapter 12.

Working with Symbols

Since a dot journal is pretty much an offshoot of bullet journal, the basic elements are retained including those strange symbols you see next to the to-do list. They are helpful in keeping track of your progress. It's a smart way of tracking and monitoring because you can see them all in one page. With a quick look, you immediately know what you need to do.

As a recap, the following symbols are explained below.

X Task Completed

> Task Migrated

< Task Scheduled

o Event

– Note

On top of the symbols, there are also signifiers that provide context to the tasks or events.

* Priority

! Inspiration / Idea

Eye symbol means Explore

If you feel comfortable using these symbols, then you're good to go. If you find them confusing, you can create your own symbols and signifiers. Just make sure that you create a key or legend in your journal (front or back) so you can keep track of what they mean.

Layout for Form and Function

Dot journaling opened the floodgates for the creative types to come up with amazing layouts that combine fun and function.

- *Weekly Log.* This is a list of things that you need to do in the course of the week.

- *Morning/Afternoon/Evening Tasks.* This involves breaking up your tasks and events into time periods, so they are more manageable.

- *Separating Goals and Tasks.* It's important to recognize that goals are much bigger than daily tasks. Separating them can give you a sense of priority and intention. If your daily tasks lead to the achievement of your goals, then you're off to a fantastic start.

- *Lists.* Lists are not always about something you need to buy, errands to run, or chores to do. You can have a list of people who inspire you or a list of places you want to visit.

- *Tracker.* This is a type of layout that tracks the progress of your goal or habit. It can be multiple goals, but the tracker works well with a single goal because you can see your progress in just one page. They can be a daily or monthly tracker.

The layout to use will depend on the kind of daily tasks you have and the type of goal you want to accomplish. For example, if you want to lose weight or save up some money, you might want to include a tracker on top of your bullet list.

Dot Journaling is a more creative and exciting way to use a journal as a productivity tool. It combines intention, prioritization, and action and allows you to track your activities and accomplish tasks in the most efficient way possible. There is also a sense of importance to your daily tasks because they become part of a bigger goal.

Chapter 9

Getting Started

You now have a clear understanding of smart journaling and the approaches available to get you started. This chapter will help you figure out what you want to get out of journaling.

Commit to Smart Journaling

Any new project or activity can only succeed if there is a strong commitment to the cause. It's easy to abandon a project, not because it's difficult, but because there is a lack of commitment from the people involved. Having the intention is only half the battle. You should be in it for the long haul to benefit from the process. Otherwise, you will just be wasting time.

Set Your Goal

Ask yourself: *"What am I trying to achieve?"*

Take a moment to look deep within yourself and identify the areas of your life that you need to work on. Focus on the one important area that will have a consequence on the others. Smart journaling is synonymous to intentional journaling because there is a goal to be achieved. There is something that has to be accomplished. Without a goal in mind, there is no point in going through the process. So before you pick up a pen and a notebook, make sure that your goal is crystal clear.

- *Types of Goals*

  Short-Term Goals – if you are looking at achieving your goals in the near future, they are considered to be short-term goals. Though most goals are time-bound, there's really no specific rule on the number of years for the goal to be categorized as short-term. Typically, they are goals that you want to get done soon. Some examples of these goals are:

  - Purchase a television
  - Enroll in a culinary class
  - Redecorate room

  Long-Term Goals – if you expect the goals to take longer to accomplish or achieve, then you are looking at long-term goals. They are typically plotted on timeframes that are longer than a year. They require careful thought and planning. Achieving these goals could have a significant impact on your life, some may even be life-changing or career-changing. Some examples are:

- Purchase a house or property
- Become a doctor
- Save up for retirement

Stepping Stone Goals – These are transactional goals necessary to reach a bigger long-term goal. An example is paying off part of a debt

Lifetime Goals – These are goals that take a long time to achieve. They usually involve life-changing personal goals and choices that refer to your development as a person.

Knowing the types of goals enables you to distinguish one from another so that you can set them accordingly based on their complexity and the time it takes to achieve them. This way, you can easily measure your progress towards your goals.

How many goals are too many and how few are too few? The number of goals you set is really up to you. Having too many goals is fine as long as you can manage them. Every goal has a different level of complexity. If your goals are mostly complex ones, then you might struggle with managing them. If your goals comprise mostly of short-term ones, then it would be much easier to handle them simultaneously. Setting goals also entails managing expectations.

- *Use the S.M.A.R.T Model*

  You must set your goals following the SMART framework.

  o Specific. Your goal must be specific and clearly defined. To test if your goal is specific, you should answer the questions *What, Why,* and *How.*

  Example: On January 1, 2018, I will join a weight-loss program that promotes following a strict diet and exercise plan that will help me lose 10 lbs in one month.

  What: Join a weight-loss program

  Why: Lose 10 lbs in one month

  How: Following a strict diet and exercise plan

  o Measurable. The goal must have a tangible evidence to determine if it is a success or not. An example of a tangible evidence is the metrics for which to measure the goal. In the example above. The metric is the weight loss measured in pounds.

  o Achievable. Your goal must not be wild and outrageous. It must be something that can be achieved without any superhuman intervention. But take note that it has to be something that is also challenging. You must possess the skills and ability to achieve the goal. You should have the capacity to do things without causing you harm. In the example above, losing 10 lbs in a month is within a person's capacity to achieve by sheer hardwork and determination.

- o <u>Results-Focused (Realistic).</u> Your goal must focus on the outcome more than the activities to reach the outcome. It has to be realistic and sensible. In the example above, the result is the weight loss and not the individual activities that were done to get to the result.

- o <u>Time-Bound.</u> Your goal must have a time frame so that it would create a sense of urgency. It's pretty much like a deadline that you must stick to. This is not to stress you out, but to bridge the gap between the goal and the reality. Without the urgency, you are more likely to delay the achievement of the goal or abandon it altogether. In the example above, the goal of losing weight must be accomplished in one month. It gives urgency and at the same time a reasonable amount of time to succeed in the endeavor.

Using the SMART model in journal writing keeps you focused and grounded. It sets you up to succeed because you are working in a framework that guides you in the right direction. It prevents you from thinking about outlandish goals that are impossible to achieve.

To train your mind to work within the framework of SMART, here is a practice questionnaire. Ask yourself these questions every time you want to embark on a new project or goal.

My Goal:

Specific

- What will my goal accomplish?
- How will I accomplish my goal?
- Why should I accomplish my goal?

Measurable

- How will I measure the outcome?
- What are the metrics that I can put in place to measure the success of failure of the goal?
- Give at least two specific indicators or measurement.

Achievable

- Is my goal achievable given my skills and abilities?
- Have other people achieved success with the same goal?
- Do I possess the necessary skills and resources to achieve my goal?
- Will achieving the goal leave me feeling defeated or worse than I was before I started?

Results-Focused

- What would be the outcome of my goal?
- What is the benefit of accomplishing my goal?

Choose Your Approach

The types of journals were discussed in Chapter 5 to give you an idea of what possible approaches you can use to kickstart your journal writing. Your goal will indicate the kind of journal process that you will be pursuing. You're not limited to just one approach because smart journaling can include many of the approaches but in a streamlined format. It's pretty similar to Bullet Journal, but with your own customizations in place.

Get Your Tools

Journaling is not an expensive activity. It only requires a pen and a notebook or simply a Microsoft Word document. If you're a minimalist, that's all you'll ever need. But journaling also has a creative side to it. Sometimes, journals become crafts project because of the accoutrements that creative journal writers use. They use stickers, color pens, grid lines, index markers, and other add-ons that would make the experience more fun to do and more personal.

- *Pre-made Journal vs. Blank Pages*

   The type of notebook to use would depend on the approach you'll be adopting. Premade journals are those that already have built-in designs like lines, grids, calendars, or checklist, to name a few. They are essentially ready-made templates that are the same for every page. If you are creatively-challenged, then the pre-made journals would be the obvious choice. You just have to write and not do much else.

The journal with blank pages is particularly useful for those who would like to vary their journal entries because they have multiple goals in mind. It's also for those who want to create their own designs using arts and craft materials. With blank page journals, you can customize each page to include layouts, drawings, and artworks. Some people use sketchbooks because they are basically a blank canvas that they can unleash their creativity on.

If you are leaning towards using the Bullet Journal system, you would benefit from using a templated journal that has dot grid pages.

- *Writing Pens*

Any writing pen would do as long as they don't leave smear marks on most paper types. But if you want to get fancy, you can also add markers, color pens, Sharpies, and crayons to your writing arsenal.

- *Add-ons*

Journaling can get those creative juices flowing. Some people really put a lot of time and effort on beautifying their journals. It's just a way to personalize their journals. But add-ons are not just for aesthetic purposes, they are also functional. Examples include stickers, page holders, index markers, and bookmarks.

- *Electronic Journals*

An electronic journal comes with many subtypes but most commonly it will be a Microsoft Word document on your computer. The Microsoft Word Journal is essentially a private journal written through electronic means. You open a word document and type your thoughts, ideas, and description of events in the same way you would write in a notebook journal.

One drawback of MS Journals is that they're remarkably easy to edit with very little indicator that it has been edited. This makes it very easy to violate our general rule: thou shall always be honest when writing in your journal.

Some Advantages of an MS Journal

- You can input pictures with ease. You can download from the internet and just pin images there that you feel best show what you want to describe. You can also transfer images from your mobile phone to the document, giving you lots of leeway when it comes to creativity.

- Speaking of creativity, don't forget that Microsoft Word – as well as various writing platforms – provides a variety of options in how documents are written. You can change sizes, fonts, spacing, add some Word Art, add a few tables, include a chart, and so on. You don't have the same limitations as when you write a Journal on an actual notebook. If you feel like screaming, you can have all the letters caps locked. You can make them small if you're feeling insecure or shy or you can have them warbled if you're feeling confused.

- Microsoft Word also makes listing and numbering easier. There are bullet point, number, and lettering options – giving you the chance to quickly and easily comply with writing prompts.

- Another excellent advantage of an MS Journal is the relative speed of typing compared to writing. As previously discussed, a person's thoughts can be so fast that the act of writing with a pen is incredibly slow to capture all the words. Typing therefore provides a healthy medium. Your thoughts can be slowed at a pace that matches with the speed of your typing – therefore guaranteeing that you'll be able to record all your thoughts.

Also – don't be confused when I use the word "Microsoft" as a journal. This doesn't mean that you have to use only the Microsoft word software in creating your diary. Any writing platform would do that is similar to Microsoft Word.

Prepare Yourself Mentally

Journal writing is a process and you need to prepare yourself to go through the process of writing down your thoughts, ideas, and insights. You need to be in a tip-top mental state because journaling involves mental creation. If your mind is filled with anxiety, worries, and negative thoughts, there is no room to create. What you create in your mind becomes the basis of the execution of your goals. What starts out as intangible ideas could materialize into something much more tangible, so it's important to have a clear mind before you dive in.

To prepare yourself mentally, you have to:

1. Strategically Disengage. This means disengaging from your routine and finding the time and place where you can step back and clear your mind. It's essentially letting your mind have a vacation. This mini beak

allows you to drown out the noise and gain clarity. This works particularly well if your mind is getting a little too fuzzy, your emotions are getting a little out of hand, and your stamina is running low.

Here are some of the things that you can do to strategically disengage.

- Go on a short vacation by yourself to help your mind, body, and spirit to recuperate.

- Do activities that will help you regain physical energy such as exercise, sports, sleep, or go on a retreat.

- Take short breaks in between activities to break the monotony.

2. Disconnect. Social media is largely a big noise that you have to silence. The more time you spend interacting on sites like Facebook, Twitter, and Instagram, the more likely your mind would be filled with information that is not vital to your goal. The less trivial information you absorb, the less you have to weed them out from your mind.

3. Affirm. Affirmations are based on the belief "you are what you think." What this suggests is that your thoughts have the power to make things happen, but

thoughts must first be put into words then into actions. Through this, your intentions can manifest. The act of affirming serves to clear your mind from negative thoughts. It restructures the workings of the brain so that it can empower and strengthen your will. It gives a sense of assurance that what you wish for can become a reality.

You have to affirm to yourself that you can make journaling work for you. You have to believe that you can create actionable goals and achieve them.

Here are examples of affirmations to prepare yourself for the intentional journaling process:

- I am the architect of my life. I choose the elements that I allow into my life. I am in control.
- I possess the skills, intellect, and mindset to succeed in any endeavor I choose to get involved in.
- I am superior to negativity. I can overcome negative thoughts.
- I possess a creative energy that will lead me to exciting new ideas.
- I have the tools to conquer my fears. I have the capacity to triumph over challenges.

- Today, I will embark on new habits that will help me achieve my goals.

- Even though there are obstacles in my way, I know I can hurdle them because I am more than what I fear.

- Each day brings me closer to achieving my goals.

- I am blessed with a wonderful family and amazing friends. I have the support that I need to rise up to the challenges.

- The future that I envision will materialize because I deserve it.

- My life is changing for the better and I will keep it that way.

- I will wake up each day with love in my heart and clarity in mind.

You can create as many or as few affirmations as you deem necessary. Recite these affirmations to yourself to give you a good boost of confidence at the start of your day.

4. Meditate. Meditation is a fantastic pre-journaling habit because it brings you to a higher state of being that deepens your self-reflection and self-expression. It makes you more open to discovering things about yourself, your environment, and everything that surrounds you. Meditation is great at expanding your

awareness and understanding your feelings and emotions.

By combining meditation and journal writing, you open yourself up to ideas and you gain a better and deeper understanding of whatever message is presented to you.

You can use guided meditation using apps like Headspace or you can do yoga breathing exercises. It's also suggested that you alternate meditation with journal writing. For every switch, ask yourself reflective writing questions to see if your mind is clearer and sharper.

Here are examples of the questions that you can ask:

- What is my intention for journal writing?
- Did my mind and body feel any different after meditation?
- What do I want to focus on?
- What is my goal for the week, month, or year?
- What could be the possible obstacles that I would encounter while I go through the journaling process?

***

These are just some of the pre-journaling rituals that can help you get started. Some people find that praying centers them, while others find that going for a walk clears their mind. There are no strict rules when it comes to preparation. As long as it can help you gain clarity, then by all means, keep the habit.

Chapter 10

Levelling Up in Life

You know the benefits of journaling and you've chosen the journal approach to use, but you can't quite decide which aspect of your life you want to focus on. The logical way is to focus on something that needs fixing. If you're having trouble with, say, your marriage, then you might want to put more effort into addressing the issues surrounding your marriage. This area has a sense of urgency, so you need to address it immediately.

Another approach is to focus on what you think you are neglecting. An area that usually gets neglected is health and fitness. It's not the top priority for most people, but when health starts failing, it becomes a top priority.

There's also the domino effect approach where you choose one major area of focus in your life that when you improve it, other areas will also improve organically. This is a little tricky because it's hard to identify the anchor point at the onset.

The beauty of smart journaling is that you can assess your level of success or satisfaction in all areas of your life. What you write in your journal is a good indicator of where you are in your life. It's like reading an executive summary of your life so far. It's possible to simultaneously work on all major areas of your life just by keeping a journal. You do not have to choose one over the other when you have the tools to balance your life. Journal writing is that powerful.

The challenge is on how to do it without getting overwhelmed. In his bestselling book *The Miracle Morning*, author Hal Elrod introduced the concept of *Level 10 Success*. This concept supports the idea that everyone can be living their best life if they reach the level 10 in all areas of their lives. It seems like a tall order because you don't always reach that high point in one area of your life, much less in all areas of your life. Stop, right there. This kind of pessimistic thinking can sabotage your chances of succeeding.

The first step, according to Elrod, is to have an honest assessment of yourself where you are now. If you are able to answer this question, you'll know what you need to work on.

Elrod suggests determining the 10 major areas of your life that you want to focus on. For every major area, you have to rate it from 1 to 10, which signifies your level of satisfaction; 1 being least satisfied and 10 being most satisfied. This exercise will give you a quick assessment of your life and you can figure out the areas that need your attention.

Now, here's where the fun part begins. Under each major area, write 10 goals that you want to achieve. It doesn't matter if the goals are short-, medium-, or long-term, the important thing is you write down your goals that follow the SMART model discussed in Chapter 10.

Here's an example of what this exercise can result in:

Note that the goals listed below are in their condensed format for clarity. In reality, the goals are much more detailed because they follow the SMART model.

1) Family and Friends (Relationships)
    1. Take the family on a trip to a foreign country
    2. Touch base with close friends who I have not seen in years.
    3. Answer text messages from family and friends with urgency.
    4. Call parents more often (every other day) to check up on them.
    5. Make plans with friends once a week
    6. Make plans with my brother and sister.
    7. Schedule a night out with girlfriends.
    8. Take mom shopping.
    9. Take dad golfing.
    10. Play video games with kids.

2) Personal Growth and Development
    1. Learn photo and video editing software
    2. Learn a new language (French).
    3. Go on a retreat
    4. Attend a TED talk

5. Read one fiction book every week.
6. Read one self-help or empowering book once a month
7. Learn a new skill: gardening
8. Keep up with my daily journal writing to achieve small and big goals
9. Attend seminars or workshops to improve writing skills
10. Surround myself with positive people

3) Career

1. Write and publish a book
2. Attend a writing seminar
3. Create a YouTube Channel and gain 1,000 followers in one month
4. Start a podcast
5. Create a website
6. Create and maintain a blog
7. Create viral content
8. Generate passive income
9. Create training videos
10. Create a sustainable business

4) Spiritual

1. Meditate regularly / daily
2. Develop healthy habits to clear the mind
3. Interact with people who share the same beliefs on spirituality
4. Commit to a Yoga schedule
5. Practice mindfulness
6. Keep a gratitude journal
7. Read books on the subject of spirituality
8. Join groups that promote spiritual awakening
9. Be one with nature / go on a nature trip at least once a month
10. Be mindful of others' feelings

5) Financial

1. Pay off credit card debt
2. Restructure existing debt
3. Increase my monthly savings

4. Buy a big-ticket item with cash
5. Consult a financial advisor
6. Invest in gold and silver
7. Set aside more money for the kids' college fund
8. Keep track of my expenses
9. Purchase a property for investment
10. Stay away from high-risk investment opportunities (e.g. Bitcoin, tech stocks)

6) Marriage

1. Date night once a week
2. Go on a holiday just the two of us (second honeymoon)
3. Listen more to my partner
4. Be more sensitive to my partner's needs
5. Go on a romantic walk
6. Go to the gym together/ exercise together
7. Let my partner go out with friends once a week
8. Tell partner "I love you" everyday
9. Spend quality time in the bedroom (no phone, tablets, TV)
10. Alternate cooking and household chores

7) Health and Fitness

1. Run a marathon
2. Detoxify once a week
3. Follow a healthy diet plan
4. No sugar for one month
5. Get back to playing sports
6. Do intermittent fasting
7. Go on regular medical and dental check up
8. Stop drinking soda for good
9. Get 6 to 8 hours of sleep
10. Rehydrate (at least 8 glasses of water daily)

8) Fun and Recreation

1. Watch a live comedy show
2. Watch a movie once a week
3. Watch a sporting event
4. Go on a food trip
5. Visit another country

6. Play video games with the kids
7. Drive a sports car
8. Attend the San Diego Comic Con
9. Eat at a Michelin star restaurant
10. Watch a concert

9) Religion

1. Go to church regularly
2. Get involved in church activities
3. Pray regularly
4. Teach kids about the teachings of the church
5. Do outreach work organized by church groups
6. Attend Bible studies
7. Visit Rome, Italy
8. Go on a pilgrimage to Jerusalem with mom
9. Study theology to gain deeper understanding of the church's teachings
10. Go to confession

10) Charity

1. Donate to charities
2. Volunteer at dog shelter
3. Get involved in feeding programs
4. Donate to a GofundMe campaign
5. Volunteer at a Boys & Girls Club
6. Buy Girls' Scout cookies
7. Foster dogs until they're ready for adoption
8. Offer a free online class/ tutorial
9. Help parents and siblings pay off debt
10. Volunteer at the local library

***

From these lists of goals under main areas of focus, you can get an idea of what you really want to achieve. This activity is not an end in itself, but merely a way to exercise the mind to think from general to specific. As you keep doing this, you'll find that your list will get shorter because you are eliminating the things that don't matter all that much to you. You'll end up with a streamlined list of goals that is actionable and achievable.

The next chapters will introduce more exercises that will condition the mind to think strategically and deliberately. The goal is to create a mental inventory, determine your current situation, categorize your main areas of focus, get rid of non-essentials, and focus on the things that matter to you. When you have figured all these things out, your journal writing will be smart, fun, enjoyable, efficient, and effective.

Chapter 11

Brain Training and Linking Up Goals

Brain training exercises allow you to process information faster and more efficiently. It also boosts your memory and mental core abilities. More importantly, you're able to make rational decisions and disregard distractions. In general, it's an awesome way to combat against declining cognitive function.

What does that have to do with smart journaling?

Journaling is writing your thoughts and ideas. Sometimes, you feel like you're not getting a lot of writing done because your brain is not cooperating. It's like you're having a serious case of brain fog, where you experience mental confusion, lack of focus, and poor recall. It would be impossible to keep a journal if you're in that state of mind. That's why brain exercises are necessary to keep the brain in good shape. According to Professor Sherry Willis of University of Texas, brain training makes people more efficient in doing tasks even as simple as writing down to-do lists or grocery list to much more complex task like operating machineries.

With that said, you'd want the brain exercises to complement your journal writing. This chapter trains your brain through several exercises that link up to your journal writing.

Daily Writing Prompts

The purpose of the writing prompt is to give you focus because you are able to develop a perspective on an idea, situation, a person, or event. Prompts are questions or instructions that are created to encourage you to think in specific terms. The prompts should align with your journal writing. If you intend to write a gratitude journal, your prompts should relate to things that you are grateful for. It's essentially pushing yourself to go in the direction that you want to go. This way, you can actually maximize the benefits of doing daily prompts.

Take a look at how some of the main areas of focus in Chapter 10 are used to illustrate some examples of writing prompts:

Goal: Improve Relationship with Family and Friends

Prompts

- How is your relationship with your parents at this point in your life?

- When was the last time you called your parents? What did you talk about?

- Do you have a family tradition that you no longer participate in?

- Do you still keep in touch with old friends? When was the last time you had face-to-face contact?

- How often do you spend quality time with your kids?

- Do you feel guilty about working all the time?

Goal: Personal Growth and Development

Prompts

- If given the chance, what skills you want to improve?

- What new skill do you want to acquire?

- Among the new technologies that emerge, which ones do you want to learn more of?

- Do you think that your personal growth is improving or stagnating? Why do you think so?

- How do you feel about self-help books?

- Do personal development seminars and talks appeal to you?

- Would you consider getting a life coach to help you succeed in life?

Goal: Career Advancement

Prompts

- Are you satisfied with the way your career is going?

- Do you think you're moving along the right career path?

- Has the thought of changing career occurred to you?

- Do you have the necessary skills and abilities to switch to a different career?

- Do you think you have the tools necessary to succeed in your chosen career path?

- Have you thought about the earning opportunities online?

- Do you work in a toxic environment?

- What new interests have you discovered?

Goal: Spiritual Awakening

Prompts

- Does your spirituality guide you through life?

- Have you experienced a spiritual awakening?

- Does your spirituality help ground you?

- What do you do to clear your mind?

- Do you practice mindfulness?

- Has spirituality influenced the way you interact with other people?

Goal: Financial Independence

Prompts

- What is the biggest obstacle that's stopping you from being financially independent?

- How important is financial health to you?

- Do you have other sources of income aside from your salary?

- Are you taking steps to keep your credit score high?

- Have you considered using cash more than credit cards?

- Do you splurge when you have extra income?

- How do you describe your relationship with money?

- What investment opportunities do you want to pursue?

Goal: Happy Marriage

Prompts

- How do you keep the romance alive after years of being together with your partner?

- How happy are you with your marriage?

- What are some aspects of your marriage that you need to work on?

- How has other aspects of your life affected your marriage?

- What do you do when there is turmoil in the marriage?

- Do you think it's necessary to have a "me" time even when you're in a marriage?

- Does your partner make an effort to spend quality time together or do you do all the work?

- How has your marriage and sex life changed after having kids?

Goal: Improve Health and Fitness

Prompts

- What activities do you think would help improve your physical and mental health?

- Do you think you need to change your eating habits?

- What new health regimen would you be willing to try out?

- Does going to the gym intimidate you?

- What fitness activity do you want to include in your daily routine?

- Have you achieved your ideal weight for your age and body type and build?

- Do you feel like your neglecting the health and fitness aspect of your life?

Goal: Enjoy Life with More Fun and Recreation

Prompts

- Do you take life too seriously that you don't have fun anymore?

- When was the last time you went out to have fun with your friends?

- What's your guilty pleasure?

- What recreational activities do you engage in when you want to destress?

- How do you feel about extreme sports? Are you willing to try it?

- Are you the type who feels guilty when you're having too much fun while others are stuck in their jobs?

- How often do you go out for fun?

Goal: Improve Religious Practice

Prompts

- Do you practice your religion as strictly as the church expects you to?

- Do you get involved in church activities?

- What is your contribution to the local church?

- Are you making effort to increase your religious learning?

- Is confession important to you? When was the last time you went into a confession?

Goal: Give Back to Society through Charity

Prompts

- Do you think you're giving back enough to your community or society?

- Does involvement in charitable works make you feel happy and fulfilled?

- What charitable organizations do you wish to help?

- Is donating to charity enough or do you feel you need to give more?

- How do you feel about helping a stranger financially?

- What do you think about crowdfunding sites for charitable contributions?

- Do you donate anonymously, or you want everyone to know that you helped a charitable institution?

***

These prompts are by no means exhaustive. They are provided to guide you in your journal writing. Some questions may not apply to you, but you can always tweak the questions to be more appropriate to your experiences. The beauty of these prompts is that they trigger other questions that you otherwise would not think of if you just go freewriting. It opens up new topics, themes, and ideas to extend your writing prompts. You'd be amazed at how effective prompts are in making your mind receptive to new ideas.

Writing daily for 10 minutes using these prompts can help you structure your journal writing. By the time you sit down and start your journal, you're already clear on what goals you need to prioritize, what needs to go, and what actions you must do to achieve your daily goals.

Writing Sprints

A writing sprint is a timed writing exercise. Set your timer for five minutes and write what comes to mind until the time expires. Freewriting seems too unstructured and will probably get you nowhere, but the one thing it can accomplish is to develop a writing habit. The time gives a sense of urgency that makes you think quickly and efficiently. This is a great exercise because you're writing down your thoughts and, in the process, you're discovering the things that are occupying space in your mind. You'll realize the amount of rubbish that takes up space, but you also discover worthwhile ideas.

If you want a little more structure, you can use prompts for your writing sprint. Another option would be to have a topic or theme to write about and just run with it. You can do writing sprints when you feel stuck and cannot move forward in your writing. This is particularly useful when your writer's block rears its ugly head. The time factor really gets the adrenaline pumping because you know that you have a limited time for writing things down. It can be an exhilarating exercise because once you start, the ideas will just keep flowing and you'll find that your hand cannot keep up with your brain. And once the timer expires, you'd feel a sense of fulfillment upon seeing and reading what you had written.

Writing One Sentence

This is one of the most fun exercises to do when you don't feel like writing tons of words. Writing one sentence each day is a practice in brevity. Most of the time, the things you want to say can be summed up in one sentence. And that's all it really takes to communicate a message. With this exercise, you think of more ideas long after you've jotted down your one sentence.

If you can write a sentence that describes your thoughts or what you're truly feeling, then you can streamline your journal writing. Bullet journaling and dot journaling are minimalist and streamlined forms of journal writing and they are super efficient and work so well with any approach you use. If you are keen on utilizing a straight to the point approach to journal writing, this exercise will fit you to a T.

Creating Lists

Many people like to read top 10 lists or watching videos that have countdowns because they find them interesting. But did you know that creating lists is not just a fun exercise, but it also has some real benefits? A list moves us into action. Just think of the To-Do list and the grocery list — just by looking at them, you know straight away what you need to prioritize. It's like your brain compartmentalizes the items you need to buy or the tasks you need to get things done.

If you think about it, creating lists actually solves the problem of procrastination. This is especially true for big tasks with different phases or smaller segments. You are able to tackle the task without being overwhelmed because you are able to manage the small tasks easily. You get to accomplish things in small batches, which gives you room to breathe, recharge, and recover.

Lists are not limited to grocery lists or task lists. It can be a list of rules you need to remember, a list of unsung heroes you want to pay respect to, a list of virtues you want in a mate — and the list goes on. The more you think about it, the more you realize that lists actually provide organization and structure to a world of chaos. It's something that you need if you are trying to balance your life by setting different goals for different areas of focus.

Problems and Solutions

This exercise is really simple. You identify a problem and then think of possible solutions. The answers will not come easy, but if you have options, you can weigh each of them and select the best possible solution. It's an empowering exercise that can help you plan your next moves to actually execute the chosen solution.

Reflecting on Inspirational Quotes

Inspirational quotes are usually straightforward, but some quotes have underlying meanings. In any case, reflecting on them is a good brain exercise. These quotes are encouraging and the more you reflect on them, the more empowering they become. Choose a quote that speaks to you in a profound way and reflect on its message and see how it relates to your life. It enables you to look deep into yourself and make an honest assessment of where you are at and determine where you want to go in the future.

Reaching Milestones

This exercise has two elements: a) recording milestones and b) aiming for milestones.

Milestones are significant achievements in life. You can describe your milestones in as much detail as you possibly can and describe how you felt about achieving them. This exercise not only makes you happy, but it also makes you optimistic about the future. This is particularly useful if you want to set long-term goals (because milestones usually take time to achieve).

Mind Mapping

A mind map is a diagram used to organize information or processes visually. It's a hierarchical map that shows how parts of the process are related to one another. Creating one can help you see the bigger picture. If you have a big, complex goal in mind, but don't know how to execute a plan to achieve it, you can create a mind map to see how each part connects to the others. If you know how the moving parts work, you can design your course of action with less difficulty.

Making Creative Entries

Sometimes, when the words won't come and sentences don't flow the way you want them to, the best thing to do is to get creative by drawing, sketching, or coloring. If you look at how people are writing their journals nowadays, you'll find either works of art or doodles. The journal becomes a canvas for their creativity. They are expanding and extending the use of journal writing to include graphics, colors, stickers, and other crafts materials.

The simple journal can transform to colorful pages with vibrant designs and fascinating entries. Creative people use it as an outlet, but instead of using words, they use lines, shapes, diagrams, and sketches. What they can't put into words, they use signs and symbols. So when they get back to it, the entries speak to them in visual language.

Today I Learned (TIL)

You can find out more about *Today I Learned* in the aggregator site Reddit.com. It's where people submit posts about what they learned on a particular day. The posts are essentially a list of little-known factoids that they find fascinating. If you're a trivia junkie, it's a great place to hang out online.

Today I Learned has an important application in journal writing because it can be modified to become a productivity tool. In fact, many tech programmers make use of *Today I Learned* to record their daily learnings about coding or tech stuff. What started out as a small list became a log of all learnings over time. They can refer to them when they get stuck or when they needed a way out of a rut.

It can be a great brain exercise or a daily journal prompt. In Reddit.com, the topics vary, but if you want to use it as part of a daily journal, you have to choose topics that relate to your interests and to your goals. This way, you're learning new things that link directly to what you're trying to achieve.

There are many ways to do this. You can put post one each day on each page of your journal or create a TIL journal separately. Going for the latter is recommended because there will be a lot of entries to be recorded over time. It will save you a lot of time going back and forth journal pages when you have a journal dedicated for just TIL journaling.

Here are some examples of TIL entries:

Say, you're a writer who wants to pursue a career as a novelist, you can collect TIL factoids to inspire you, move you, and help you learn writing techniques.

2018 Today I learned...

January 1: The manuscript of Harry Potter by J.K. Rowling was rejected 12 times by different publishers. Bloomsbury picked it up and paid Rowling a measly advance of £1,500. The book series has sold 450 million copies worldwide.

January 2: Crime writer Agatha Christie taught herself to read at the age of 8 because her mother didn't want her to learn to read.

January 3: Huffington Post does not pay guest bloggers and contributors to their site.

January 4: For English speakers, adjectives must be written in this order: *opinion-size-age-shape-colour-origin-material-purpose Noun*

You get the idea.

If you look at the entries, they are trivial at its best. But if you examine them closer, you'll find that there are lessons to be learned from the entries. For the January 1 entry, it's not really about J.K. Rowling or Harry Potter. It's about perseverance, determination, and never giving up. For the January 2 entry, it's not about the bad choices of Agatha Christie's mother. It's about Agatha's sheer determination to learn how to read. These two entries are both inspiring and motivating. The last two entries give out two different lessons. It's just a matter of looking beneath the surface to find valuable life lessons.

Negative to Positive Thinking

The brain has the natural tendency to dwell on the negatives. This is why you remember insults, abuses, invectives, and other negative actions that were hurled towards you in the past. The brain has a negativity bias because it is more receptive to negative stimuli. The brain just can't help it. It's just more drawn to undesirable things.

It has to do with the brain's propensity to keep you out of harm's way. It's part of our survival process. You are hardwired to notice danger because your brain has developed a system to alert you when danger is coming so that you can immediately take action to avoid it. This evolutionary phenomenon has an effect on how people act towards others and how they behave in their relationships. It also affects how people evaluate their actions and make decisions in life.

The challenge is to keep the balance between positive and negative thoughts. Since you dwell on more negative events than the positive ones, you should learn to practice positive thinking techniques to keep the balance. Research studies have shown four proven ways to make this happen.

1. Take pleasure in the good things that happen in your life. Studies show that even though negative thoughts and events are indelibly etched in our mind because the brain is hardwired to do so, it only takes between five and twenty seconds to absorb positive events.

   If you experience positive things in life, take a moment to savor the joy and happiness you feel when wonderful things happen. The positive experience will extend to all your senses and the brain will begin to remember them. The more you do this, the more you can drown out the negative thoughts.

2. Be grateful. Gratitude always makes you feel good. Expressing gratitude promotes positive feelings. Gratitude means being thankful for all the things that you receive, whether tangible or intangible, good or bad. When you're grateful, you recognize that the

source of the goodness lies beyond yourself and you acknowledge that you are connected to a higher being more powerful than yourself. As a result, you forge better relationships with others and it improves your overall well-being.

When you are in a state of gratitude, you can train your brain to dwell on the positive events rather than the negative ones. Keeping a gratitude journal helps tremendously in promoting an overall positive feeling.

- Write down three good or positive things that happened during your 24-hour day.
- Celebrate the positive events. It doesn't have to be flashy or extravagant.
- Recognize the small triumphs each day and life will change in a significant way.

3. Tune out. If you can disconnect from social media, you can easily tune out the negative events that are reported in the news everyday. The sad part is that in the news cycle, the negative events are given priority and are sensationalized. This forces those who watch to consume violent and depressing news.

The good part is that you don't have to watch the negative reports all day. You can switch off and tune out for 24 hours or 48 hours. If you can't help it, then just watch the headlines, then switch to shows that focus on the positive side of life. They may be few and far in between, but there are shows that inspire viewers more than appall them. When you're able to tune out, you exposed yourself to more positive events.

4. Distance yourself for more accurate reactions and judgment. It is in people's nature to perceive new things as threats. As a result, they act according to their instincts rather than thinking things through. Of course, there are cases wherein you should let your instincts prevail in order to avoid real harm.

   In some cases, however, you need to distance yourself from the event to make an accurate interpretation of what had transpired so that you can act appropriately. Journaling allows you to do this as you put your thoughts and ideas on paper.

   Before acting based on emotions, you must be able to gather information so that you can make an accurate judgement of the situation. This will not only prevent negative things from happening, it will also improve and nurture your relationships.

These are ways through which you can change your perspective and you can begin to manage the way you consume or think about negative events. You are not always in harm's way, so there's no need to overreact. You can keep negative thoughts at bay if you condition our brains to look for positive events more often.

***

There are certainly more pre-journaling exercises that you can explore, but these are some of the most popular ones. The purpose is not just to jumpstart your brain, it also compels you to start a writing habit. It prepares you to become committed to the process and to believe that the system will work for you. Journal writing can be demanding, but it can be tons of fun as well.

Try the exercises discussed in the chapter and see which ones you'd like to use in your journal writing. The interesting part here is that some of these exercises are being used as journal entries themselves. So, you'd find people keeping creative journals to track their goals and organizing their lives. It's really a matter of choosing the combination of tools and linking them up to your intentions and purpose.

You will find that your journal will contain many of the elements discussed here. Your journal can be as flashy as you want it to be. On the flip side, you can choose to go the minimalist route and be satisfied with old-fashioned writing. Either way you choose, you've already set yourself up for success because you are journaling with a purpose.

Chapter 12

Who's Afraid of Pre-Made Templates?

You've learned about Bullet Journal and Dot Journaling, but you're not keen on adopting both systems. What now? Do you just find another system or just give up journaling altogether? Well, abandoning journaling is just crazy talk. There's always a solution to even the most difficult problems. If you're the type who works more efficiently when there is a structure, then forget about getting blank journals. Instead, get those pre-made template journals that you need to fill in.

Templated journals already have prompts in them and you just have to fill in the blanks. Then, if you are already comfortable with that system, you can slowly but surely modify the structure and prompts to suit your needs. No one is rushing you, so take your time to get used to the system and believe in the process.

Flexibility is the key in journal writing. You can start with a template and gradually work your way into customization. The important thing is to start journaling as soon as you're able to organize your thoughts. As you go through the process, you'll find that a pre-made template can be limiting. You'll realize that you need to do more than just fill in the blanks or finish sentences. It's always a learning process so it's all right to start small and work your way to bigger things.

Although it is recognized that pre-made templates have limitations, they are very helpful to people who can't seem to stick to journal writing. Journal writing requires commitment and not many people have the will and determination to commit to a daily process. There are pre-made templates that are designed with the purpose of making people commit without requiring extra time and effort. Creators make it easy for users to finish entries in as little as five minutes. With that said, here are some pre-made templates that are worth checking out.

1. The Five-Minute Journal

Created by Intelligent Change, the Five-Minute Journal is perhaps one of the most popular pre-made journal templates available in the market. The creator claims to use the science of positive psychology to create the prompts and questions. It focuses on the positive things in life so people feel more grateful for the things they have. There's a renewed sense of appreciation in life, which promotes better physical and mental health.

The journal structure is designed to boost happiness in just five minutes each day. It has two main sections. The first one is the morning routine (indicated by the symbol of the sun in the upper left-hand corner of the page). It gives you the opportunity to set the tone of how the day is going to go. It starts with a positive note and locks in your intentions for the day.

The second section is the night routine (indicated by the symbol of a quarter moon). This lets you assess how the day went and asks you how you could have made it better so that you can have an even better day tomorrow.

The Five-Minute Journal starts each page with an inspirational quote from different personalities who have succeeded in their respective careers. Then it shows the prompts and the questions that must be filled in and answered in just five minutes.

It looks like this:

Morning Routine

The obstacle is an advantage, not adversity. The enemy is any perception that prevents us from seeing this. - Ryan Holiday

I am grateful for...

1._____
2._____
3._____

What would make today great?

1._____
2._____
3._____

Daily Affirmations. I am...

1._____
2._____
3._____

Evening Routine

Three Amazing Things That Happened Today

1._____

2._____

3._____

How could I have made today even better?

1._____

2._____

3._____

As you can see from the structure and format, the journal is easy to do, and it doesn't take a lot of your time, so you could do this repeatedly without getting overwhelmed or feeling burdened by the writing. The sheer simplicity makes it a brilliant way to start journal writing.

2. The Freedom Journal

Another popular pre-made journal template is The Freedom Journal created by John Lee Dumas. The journal guides you to accomplish your main goal in just 100 days. It is based on a scientific approach, so you know that you are progressing systematically. It is goal-centric and methodical. Perhaps one of the reasons why people don't accomplish their goals is they are not using the appropriate approach for the kind of goals that they are pursuing. This is a common problem that is hardly addressed by pre-made journal templates.

In general, there seems to be a lack of understanding of the scientific approach that's why some people fail to recognize what they are doing wrong. If there is an effective process in place, success couldn't be far behind.

The Freedom Journal is designed with entrepreneurs in mind, but it does not mean that it can't be used by other folks. It is a cross between a self-help book and an inspirational and motivational prompt. It has a no-nonsense approach that lets you create big goals and achieve them realistically.

The focus is on one major goal. It could be something wild and seemingly unattainable. But, if the right framework and attitude are applied, you'd be surprised at how easy it can be achieved. Successful people are determined to reach their big goals.

The approach works because it breaks down a big goal into manageable chunks. It does not make you feel overwhelmed because you are accomplishing small goals that are crucial to the accomplishment of your number one goal. You would not feel like you're constantly moving mountains and battling insurmountable odds because you are handling something that you can manage with ease.

Since it is based on a scientific approach, you are being trained to think methodically. If you are a scatterbrain, this would give you some discipline to finish small tasks and build upon them without feeling inundated by the next set of goals. It's a great guide to keep you moving in the right direction.

The key to accomplishing goals, no matter how ambitious they appear to be, is in the goal creation process. The SMART goal-setting process discussed in Chapter 9 is the critical component of the process. Without this crucial first step, it would be very difficult to move forward. The journal could not emphasize this enough and the more you are reminded of it, the more likely it would stick.

There is an element of accountability when you journal following the Freedom Journal process. This serves as an extra layer of guarantee that you are taking concrete steps to achieve your goals. In a way, it makes your commitment more tangible.

The Freedom Journal utilizes the 10-day sprint exercises with a corresponding quarterly review. This means that the 100 days are broken down into 10-day sprints. This allows you to evaluate what you have done in that short amount of time. This enables you to reflect on what's working and what's not.

Once you are able to identify the shortcomings, you can think of ways to improve your process in the next sprint. It's like stepping up the ladder and feeling that you are improving in tremendous ways even if you are accomplishing the smallest of goals.

Templates, in general, are a little rigid, but the Freedom Journal allows flexibility in that you can reflect on your progress and make the necessary changes as you see fit. You can go beyond the prompts if you feel like you're being held back.

The Freedom Journal is useful to people who are willing to put in the time and effort to make the process work. It's not some magical process that automatically makes your dreams come true if you buy the journal. The journal can be very effective if you commit to it and religiously follow the daily process.

3. The Mastery Journal

The popularity of The Freedom Journal prompted John Lee Dumas to create The Mastery Journal. This journal caters to people who are struggling with productivity, discipline, and focus. If you understand the basic principles of journal writing but are having difficulty focusing or just don't have the discipline to go through the process, you need something that can help you address these issues first. It would be difficult to start journal writing if you have not mastered the essential skills needed to make journaling work.

Just like The Freedom Journal, The Mastery Journal promises a significant change in your life in just 100 days. It has the following features:

Morning Routine. This exercise allows you to get into good habits that can start your day right.

Daily Sessions. This daily exercise is comprised of timed sessions where you are focusing on one thing only.

Self-Evaluation. This involves assessing yourself and identifying your strengths and weaknesses.

10-Day Recap. The recap lets you identify what's working and what's not. This is to allow you to make the necessary steps to change what you're doing wrong. It's in this section where you make the adjustments.

Affirmations. This allows you to develop a positive attitude and a confident self. Journal writing and working towards a goal require a positive mindset. Without it, it would be easy to give up when you are presented with a setback.

Inspiring Quotes. Quotes are reminders of how great men and women beat the odds while aspiring for greatness or just simply achieving goals. They've been through what you are going through. Their experiences and advice might just be the boost that you need to keep going.

The Mastery Journal focuses on enhancing the skills necessary to achieve your goals quickly. It builds character because it instils discipline. It puts a spotlight on productivity and focus because they are the building blocks on which goals are achieved.

4. The SELF Journal

Created by BestSelf, The SELF Journal is similar in many ways with The Freedom Journal and The Mastery Journal in that it focuses on goal setting. The difference is that The SELF Journal focuses on organizing your daily tasks to align them to your goals. It believes that aligning daily output with life goals is the key to ending procrastination and distractions.

It follows a structure that keeps your enthusiasm high. It keeps you motivated because you're organizing your schedules and lining them up so that the tasks that you are finishing up lead to the achievement of your goals.

The journal structure ensures that the daily targets are aligned with the goal. The progress can easily be monitored because completing a task brings you closer to achieving the goal that you truly desire. The SELF Journal lets you plan your day to get results. You are given 13 weeks to complete your tasks and achieve your goals.

5. The Emergent Task Planner

The Emergent Task Planner is not a full planner like the previously discussed pre-made journal templates, but it can be used in conjunction with the templates or you can use a version of it and incorporate it to your existing journal format. Using it can get your day into a great start. It makes you feel like you're already accomplishing something just by filling in the blanks and setting up the planner.

Just like The Freedom Journal, it is methodical and task-focused. It has three elements that are the cornerstones of productivity. It makes you focus on the small yet important tasks. It makes you prioritize the tasks based on the impact they have on your day and ultimately on the achievement of your higher goals.

The next important element of The Emergent Task Planner is the assessment phase. It lets you estimate the time you need to complete the tasks. It's pretty flexible because you set a realistic time frame to complete the tasks. You are not burdened with tight deadlines that are unreasonably imposed. This time, visualization helps you to see how much time you have left in the day, so you can make further plans or adjust them accordingly.

David Seah designed The Emergent Task Planner to have a concrete goal tracker. Seah recognizes the importance of usability and ease of use. The design just helps you remain grounded and realistic, so you are not setting yourself up for a spectacular failure.

The ability to track your progress by blocking out the time in the day grid sets this apart from other planners because it gives a sense of how much you have in a day so you can allot some time to unexpected tasks or possible distractions and interruptions. It's a practical approach to organizing and task planning. This tool is particularly useful for people who like to keep track of their to-do lists and daily tasks.

These are just some of the well-known pre-made journal templates that you use. You can search online for free templates, so you can get started. They're basically like bikes with trainer wheels on. They guide you through each step and let you go when you're ready to start your journey.

Chapter 13

Application

There are many concepts, ideas, theories, and approaches to smart journaling that are presented here in this book, and it would be understandably difficult to use them all at once. To apply the learnings presented in the chapters, the practical thing to do is just choose that applies to your situation.

For minimalists, the Bullet Journal approach would most likely be preferable. If you easily get distracted, having a streamlined journaling process would help you focus on the daily tasks that have bearing on your short-term goals.

Here's a good example of how Bullet Journaling is applied:

For the pre-journaling phase, the following mental and writing exercises were used:

- Daily prompts

- Daily affirmations

- Gratitude List

- Brain Dump (Writing down anything that comes to mind, without thinking if they are going to be relevant to the daily tasks or goals.

- Goal Brainstorming (to figure out short-term goals, long-term goals, and lifetime goals)

For the journaling phase:

- SMART Goal-Setting

- Identify a short-term goal.

- Plan tasks that contribute to the achievement of the short-term goal.

- Apply rapid logging.

- Use the symbols and signifiers learned in Bullet Journal and Dot Journaling.

- Write "Today I learned..." everyday. It doesn't have to be related to any task or goal.

- Create a tracker and include it in the journal.

Here's how a minimalist Bullet Journal entry would look like:

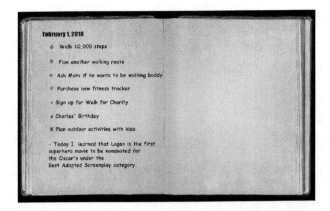

A daily tracker is added to monitor daily tasks relating to the fitness goals:

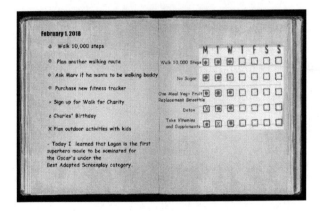

As you can see, the journal is neat, clean, and very straight to the point. It fits the person's purpose and addresses some of the issues she faces when journaling. This is a goal-centric daily journal where the owner works towards achieving her goal by completing daily tasks.

A daily tracker was added to see how she was progressing with her fitness goals. A quick look at the tracker shows what areas the owner is neglecting or not doing as religiously as she intended to. From this quick evaluation, she is motivated to do better on the following week.

It's easier to make adjustments when you are able to see what needs adjusting. It is recommended to have a tracker for a single goal or multiple daily tasks. It could be for financial goals, weight goals, health goals, or any goal that can be tracked.

Your journal would most likely be completely different from what is illustrated here and that is totally fine (and encouraged). It has to fit your intentions, your habits, and your personality. If you create it based on these elements, you're more likely to keep a journal and use it for a long time.

Now, it's your turn to get started making your very own journal.

Conclusion

When you write down things on paper, you get a sense of what you really want to do, and you set your goals accordingly. Using the *SMART* method for goal-setting makes even the most abstract of ideas become tangible. The goal becomes real and for every task you accomplish, you are slowly but surely getting closer to achieving your goals.

The pre-journaling phase is just as important as the journal writing itself because it conditions you to journal with a purpose. It makes you mentally, physically, and spiritually ready to go through the process and make it a regular writing journey.

The brain training in the form of writing prompts and mental exercises is necessary to get you in that space where you can gain clarity and focus. They do a great job of decluttering the mind from unnecessary information. As a result, you get more space to take in more relevant information and process them accordingly.

The actual journal writing itself is a fun way to track your daily progress in relation to the goals you have set out for yourself. Daily writing makes you more aware of your actions and you deliberately do things that you know are good for you.

The journal is also a way to review your life at a particular point in time. You can look back at the pages and you can determine if you are making good progress or getting stuck with procrastination. You can immediately gauge how far you have gone or how much more you need to do.

When you keep track of your activities through journaling, you can also see your mistakes and the drawbacks that are delaying you from achieving your goals. Mistakes happen, but the great thing about journaling is that you can rectify whatever mistakes you've committed. There is so much learning in journal writing, whether about yourself or your attitudes toward situations and events.

Smart journaling, like most productivity tools, is not for everyone. Some people prefer not to record every activity they do each day and just coast through life the way they see fit. But there are some people who are hopelessly disorganized. They lose the ability to focus on the important things that matter to them. Without focus, it would be difficult to set goals, much less achieve them. Smart journaling gives you the clarity and focus that you need to live a well-intentioned life.

Resources

References

Awaken The Giant Within by Tony Robbins

The Artist's Way by Julia Cameron

The Miracle Morning by Hal Elrod

The ONE Thing by Gary Keller and Jay Papasan

Morning Pages by Julia Cameron

Journals

Bullet Journal by Ryder Carroll http://bulletjournal.com

Dot Journaling—A Practical Guide by Rachel Wilkerson Miller http://www.rachelwmiller.com/

The Morning Routine Journal by Mackenzie Reed: https://www.amazon.com/dp/B07883H29G

The 2018 Success Journal by Mackenzie Reed: https://www.amazon.com/dp/B0785767LW

The 5-Minute Journal by Intelligent Change https://www.intelligentchange.com

The Freedom Journal by John Lee Dumas

https://thefreedomjournal.com/

The Mastery Journal by John Lee Dumas

https://www.themasteryjournal.com/

The SELF Journal by https://bestself.co/products/self-journal

The Emergent Task Planner by David Seah

https://davidseah.com/node/the-emergent-task-planner/

13367282R00070

Made in the USA
Lexington, KY
30 October 2018